Where Does **Water** Come From?

by C. Vance Cast
Illustrated by Sue Wilkinson

BARRON'S

Hi, I'm Clever Calvin. I'm just getting myself a glass of water at the kitchen sink. Have you ever wondered why water is so important? Have you ever wondered where it comes from?

Our planet, Earth, is covered mostly by water. For every square mile of dry land there are about three square miles of water. All forms of life—animals, plants, and people—need water to live.

Our bodies are made mostly of water—not only our blood, but even our bones, fat, organs, and muscles contain water. We have more water in our bodies than all other chemicals put together.

It is easy to see that water is important. But where does it come from?

Does water come from
the kitchen water faucet?

Does water come from
a shower?

Does water come from the washing machine?

Does water come from the lawn sprinkler?

Yes. Water does come from all these places.

But how did the water get to your house in the first place? Let's start off by explaining the *water cycle*.

When water is heated by the sun, it slowly turns into an invisible gas called *water vapor*. The vapor is lighter than air, so it rises high up into the sky. This process is called *evaporation*.

As the heated vapor rises into the sky, it cools, collects into tiny droplets or snowflakes, and forms clouds. This is called *condensation*. Sometimes the clouds may look very dark.

When colder air cools these clouds, the droplets
combine to form larger drops or flakes. Finally,
the water falls out of the clouds as *precipitation*.
Precipitation is rain, snow, sleet, or hail.

Some of the water evaporates right back into the air—
continuing the water cycle. Some of the water is
absorbed by plants that need it in order to grow.
And some of it sinks deep into the ground.

Underground water can collect in caverns, but most of it seeps down until it reaches a layer of solid material it can't go through. The water then fills the spaces between grains of sand and cracks in rocks forming an underground layer of water called an *aquifer*.

A lot of the water that stays on the surface runs off into lakes, streams, and rivers. Eventually, most of the water that falls to earth makes its way to the oceans. Even the water that goes underground finds its way to the oceans.

But where does the water that we drink and bathe with come from? One place is from underground water—the aquifers. And the other place is from lakes and rivers.

A lake that supplies water to a town or city is called a *reservoir*. A reservoir is where water is stored until it is needed.

Some reservoirs are made by putting a wall across a river. This wall is called a *dam*. The water can't go past the dam so it floods into the lowland behind it, forming an artificial lake.

Most surface water needs lots of treatment before it can be used. First, it goes to the pumping station. There it is screened to remove fish, plants, and garbage.

A chemical called *chlorine* is added to kill the bacteria. Then the water is left in a settling tank so all the dead bacteria, fine soil particles called *silt*, and other solid wastes can sink to the bottom.

The top water from the settling tank is sent to another tank where it is filtered through sand and gravel to remove any wastes that might still be in it.

In some cities, the clean water is often put through a process called *aeration*. That means it is mixed with air by forcing it into a fine spray or letting it splash down over steps. This makes the water taste and smell better.

Some cities add *fluoride* to the water to help keep our teeth in good condition.

The clean water is pumped through underground pipes called *water mains*. It may be sent directly to your house or it may be stored in a *water tower*. You probably have seen water towers. They often have the name of the town painted on them.

Water towers are higher than the buildings they supply. So, when you turn on a faucet, the water pours out because the pressure pushes it through the pipes all the way to your house.

If your city is near a big lake or river, that is where your water probably comes from. But some cities must bring in fresh water from many miles away. Although Los Angeles and New York are right beside the ocean, they can't use that water. It is too salty.

Water is brought to these cities by *aqueducts*. An aqueduct can be a big ditch or canal that is paved with stones, bricks, or concrete. It can be a tunnel deep under the ground. Or it can be pipes on top of the ground.

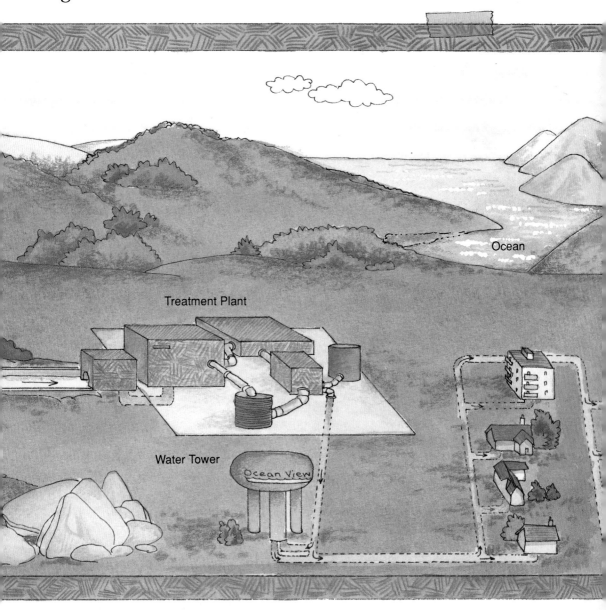

Ocean

Treatment Plant

Water Tower

Ocean View

Some cities that aren't near a lake or river get water from an aquifer. To get water from an aquifer, people must drill a deep hole called a *well*. Big machines called drilling rigs are used.

The drilled hole is then lined with pipes. When the well is finished, powerful pumps are used to draw the water out of the ground.

Water from aquifers usually is naturally filtered when the water seeps through the soil. Aquifer water is also usually free of germs, but cities may add chlorine to keep bacteria from growing in it.

Water Tower

Silver Spring

Farmers, ranchers, and people who live in the country often have their own private wells. Since the water is usually free of germs and is used right away, it generally doesn't have to be treated with chemicals.

Pumping Station

Pump

After we use the water, where does it go? It goes down the drain into the sewer.

This sewage water is going to a treatment plant where it is cleaned and treated with chemicals again. This is called *reclaimed wastewater*.

Most of the reclaimed wastewater is sent back into rivers, lakes, and oceans...

...where it can go through the whole water-cycle process of evaporation, condensation, and precipitation all over again.

So, every time you take a shower or get a glass of cold water, you can think about how the water got to your house, and what happens to it when it leaves.

Here is a fun experiment you can do.

On a hot day, fill a jar half full of water, put the lid on tight, and put the jar in the sun.

After a couple of hours, look at the inside of the jar. Do you see the tiny drops of water? How did they get there?

Some of the water evaporated, rose to the top of the jar, and then condensed back into liquid. Those are the droplets you see.

Now, draw a line on the jar
with a crayon to show where
the water level is. Remove
the lid and put the jar back
in the hot sun.

After a day, check the mark on the glass.
What happened to some of the water?
Where did it go? It evaporated into the air!

That was fun.
Lets try the
next experiment.

Clean and dry a tin can. Make sure it is very dry on the outside. Fill the can with ice cubes and let it stand for a few minutes.

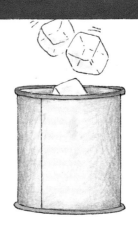

When you return to check the can, what do you see? Where has the water come from? No, the can didn't leak. What you see is condensation! When the warm water vapor in the air around the can touched the cold can, some of it changed to drops of water.

Hope you had fun. Bye for now.

Glossary

aeration The process of mixing air with water.

aqueduct A canal, tunnel, or other structure that carries water from one place to another.

aquifer The underground layer of water-soaked sand and rock that acts as a water source for a well.

condensation The process of changing from a gas (or vapor) into a solid or liquid.

chlorine A chemical added to water to kill bacteria.

dam A wall built across a stream or river to gather and store water.

evaporation The process of changing from a liquid into a gas (or vapor).

fluoride A chemical added to drinking water to help prevent tooth decay.

precipitation Water that falls from the atmosphere in the form of rain, snow, hail, or sleet.

reclaimed wastewater Used water that has been filtered and treated.

reservoir A pond or lake where water is stored for later use.

silt Fine particles of soil carried and deposited by running water.

water cycle A continuous process during which water evaporates from the earth, condenses in the air, returns to earth in the form of precipitation, evaporates again, and so on.

water main The large, underground pipe used to transport water to a neighborhood. There, it branches into smaller pipes that may branch again until they reach each individual home.

water tower An elevated tank for storing water. A pump is needed to force the water into the tank. Since the tower is higher than the buildings it supplies, the water flows down to the buildings because of gravity.

water vapor A colorless, odorless gas that forms when water evaporates.

well A hole dug into the earth for the purpose of obtaining water, oil, or natural gas.

© Copyright 1992 by Barron's Educational Series, Inc.
250 Wireless Boulevard
Hauppauge, NY 11788

International Standard Book No. 0-8120-4642-0

Library of Congress Catalog Card No. 91-35178

PRINTED IN HONG KONG
2345   4900   098765432

Library of Congress Cataloging-in-Publication Data
Cast, C. Vance.
   Where does water come from? / by C. Vance Cast ; illustrated by Sue Wilkinson.
   Summary: Answers the title question with a number of answers, such as rain, reservoirs, aquifers, and wells.
   ISBN 0-8120-4642-0
   1. Water—Juvenile literature. [1. Water supply.] I. Wilkinson, Sue (Susan), ill. II. Title.
QC920.C37   1992
551.48—dc20   91-35178